CANNONS

An Introduction to Civil War Artillery
By Dean S. Thomas

TABLE OF CONTENTS

Introduction 2
Organization and Drill 3
Parts of the Cannon 6
Manufacture of Cannon 7
Carriages 10
Types of Projectiles 16
Manufacture of Projectiles 21
Friction Primers and Time Fuses 25
6-Pounder Field Gun 27
12-Pounder Field Gun 28
Field Howitzers 31
12-Pounder Mountain Howitzer 32
Parrott Field Rifles 33
3-Inch Ordnance Rifle 39
14-Pounder James Rifle 42
12-Pounder Whitworth Rifle 43
30-Pounder Parrott Rifle 45
4.5-Inch Siege Rifle 46
24-Pounder Coehorn Mortar 47
13-Inch Seacoast Mortar 50
32-Pounder Seacoast Gun 52
Parrott Heavy Rifles, Seacoast 53
Columbiads 55
Miscellaneous 58
Artillery Implements 64
Summary of Federal Purchases 71
Bibliography 72
Table of Fire, 20-Pounder Parrott Rifle .... Back Cover

INTRODUCTION

Dotting our national military parks, monuments, and battlefields of the American Civil War are hundreds of silent artillery weapons. Most of the cannon barrels are now mounted on replica iron carriages to better weather the ravages of time. Nevertheless, these cannons that once spoke with fury are the last relics on the exact site where the death and destruction occurred during the years 1861 to 1865. The battlefield litter of broken men, muskets, and munitions has all been picked up. New growth replaces that shot to pieces or trampled during the war. Although most of the cannons were brought back to the scene of their "glory" after the establishment of historical parks, they are still visual reminders of the great tragedy — timeless memorials to the soldiers on both sides.

The subject of Civil War artillery has already filled volumes, but it is merely the intention of this writing to introduce the reader to the varied weapons, ammunition, and equipments. In addition to the more common types illustrated here, other cannons saw use during this era. For more details, please consult the suggested reading list.

In 1860, the artillery for United States land forces was divided into four classes and then further divided, depending upon its deployment and caliber.

I. GUNS — heavy weapons with long barrels to batter fortifications with shot at long range.
    A. Seacoast
    B. Siege and Garrison
    C. Field

II. HOWITZERS — shorter-barrelled guns with "chambers" in the bores for smaller powder charges. They were designed to fire shells at higher elevation over less range.
    A. Seacoast
    B. Siege and Garrison
    C. Field
    D. Mountain

III. MORTARS — short-chambered pieces used for lobbing shells at great elevation into the fortifications of the enemy.
    A. Seacoast
    B. Siege and Garrison

IV. COLUMBIADS — long-barrelled weapons combining the features of all three of the above, and were the heaviest pieces in use.

The weapons shown on the following pages are more or less categorized by deployment. Seacoast weapons were the heaviest types and were mounted in permanent fortifications on the seaboard. Siege and garrison artillery was heavier and less maneuverable than field artillery. It was used to attack (siege) or defend (garrison) fortifications and field works. Field pieces or light artillery campaigned with the troops in active operations. Mountain weapons were used in rough country where there were poor roads.

Dean S. Thomas
Arendtsville, Pa.
March 1985

ORGANIZATION AND DRILL

Civil War field artillery was organized in batteries. Although it varied from time to time, a battery in the Union army usually consisted of six of the same kind of cannons. In Confederate service, a battery was normally only four guns, and unfortunately for supply officers, may have been made up of two — even three — different kinds of weapons.

U. S. regulations prescribed a captain as a battery commander. Lieutenants commanded two gun "sections" — in battle, a battery would have a left and a right, and possibly even a center section. One gun and caisson, with their limbers, made up a platoon under a sergeant and two corporals. The sergeant was the "chief of the piece" and often the gunner. A gun crew, in addition to the gunner, consisted of seven artillerymen who were all assigned numbers for servicing the piece. In light artillery batteries, these cannoneers either marched beside their weapons or sat on the ammunition chests. All officers, sergeants, buglers, and the guidon-bearer rode horses. Horse artillerymen were all supplied with mounts. A battery at full regulation strength, including all horse holders, drivers, and other specialized functions, exceeded 100 officers and men.

Each limber in the Union army was drawn by a six-horse team. Due to a lack of horses, the Confederate army very often only used four. With spare horses included, a typical Union six-gun battery had more horses than officers and men.

A trained and disciplined battery could come into action and fire its first shot in well under one minute. Depending upon the terrain, a 14-yard space between the cannons was called for in the regulations. At Malvern Hill on July 1, 1862, however, the interval of the Union artillery was virtually hub to hub. Cannoneers took their positions as in the diagram below. At the command "Commence firing," the gunner ordered "Load." Number 1 sponged the tube. Number 2 took a round from Number 5 and placed it in the muzzle. Number 1 rammed the round home, while Number 3 held his thumb on the vent. The gunner sighted the cannon. When the gun was loaded, 3 moved to the trail and moved it left or right with the trailspike as directed by the gunner. Number 5 got another round from Number 6 or 7 at the limber where 6 cut fuses (if needed) for shell and/or case. The gunner stepped clear to the side of the piece to observe the effect of fire, and gave the command "Ready." Numbers 1 and 2 stepped clear. Number 3 punctured the cartridge bag with the vent pick. Number 4 attached the

lanyard to a friction primer and inserted the primer in the vent. Number 3 covered the vent with his left hand while 4 moved to the rear. At the gunner's command "Fire," 3 stepped clear of the wheel. Number 4 yanked the lanyard. The gunner ordered the cannon run back up and the process was repeated until the command "Cease firing."

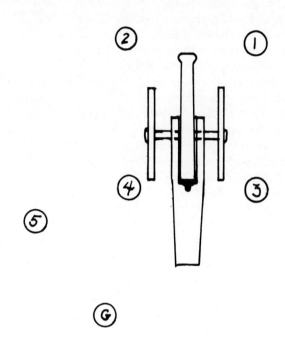

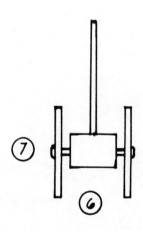

Gregory M. Breneman

Relative positions of the cannon, limber, and gun crew in action "by the manual."

Good smoothbore crews could fire two aimed shots per minute with fixed ammunition. Rifle crews were just a little slower because of the extra steps involved with loading the powder bag separate from the projectile. When firing canister, the rate of fire could be doubled, but this was often at the risk of not sponging the barrel between rounds. Sponging not only helped to cool the tube, but more importantly, it extinguished any smoldering cartridge bag remains. Against charging infantry, however, the chance of premature explosion was worth taking as opposed to the capture of the gun.

Crews for siege, garrison, and seacoast weapons were generally about the same number as field crews, even though some projectiles required at least two men to handle and load them. Depending upon the size of the mortar, the crew consisted of three, five, or more men. It could take as long as three and one half minutes to load, aim, and fire a big columbiad. Some mortars were fired at only the rate of every three to five minutes.

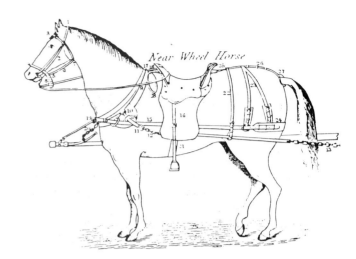

Battery horses with harness

Dead battery horses of Bigelow's 9th Massachusetts Battery at the Trostle farm, Gettysburg, Pa., July 1863.

The Federal Ringold Battery on drill with their 10-pounder Parrott rifles. The positions of the cannoneers and the intervals between the guns, limbers, and caissons are that prescribed in the "Regulations," where terrain permitted.

5

PARTS OF THE CANNON

The cannon barrel or tube was made up of a number of parts that were identified with specific names. The parts common to most Civil War barrels are shown in the drawing below. The tube is basically a U.S. 12-pounder Napoleon; however, a chamber has been added for illustration only.

a. knob
b. neck
c. vent
d. trunnion
e. muzzle swell
f. muzzle face
g. muzzle
h. rimbase
i. cascable
j. breech
k. chamber
l. bore

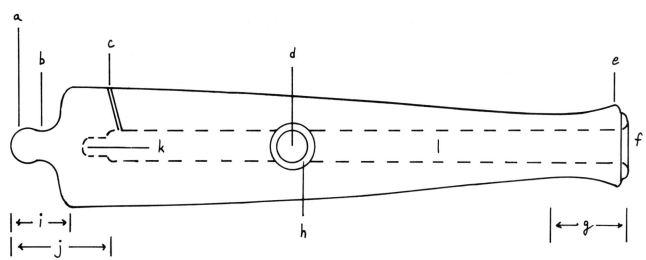

Gregory M. Breneman

MANUFACTURE OF CANNON

Cannon barrels were manufactured in a basically similar fashion to other products that were cast. A model was made, generally of hard wood, a little larger than the finished piece, but with an extension at the muzzle end termed a "sprue" or "dead-head." The sprue furnished metal to supply shrinkage and to produce greater pressure and density at the breech end of the gun. The cascable was made with a squared projection to be used in attaching machinery to give the piece a rotary motion in the boring and turning operations.

A "flask," formed of several segments of sheet iron fastened together by nuts and bolts, was the jacket or frame for the mould. The "mould" was made of hard refractory sand and clay moistened with water. To form the mould, the model was positioned in the center of the flask with the sprue end down and the moulding sand was packed firmly around it. Where the flask consisted of several pieces, they were added and the process continued until the entire model was encased. The flask was split longitudinally in the center, the model was then removed, and any needed repairs to the mould were made by hand. A "cokewash" made of water and powdered coke was brushed over the interiors of both mould halves. The wash made for a smooth surface and prevented the molten metal from adhering to the mould. The mould was then placed in an oven and baked hard.

To cast the tube, the halves of the flask were joined, and the mould placed breech down in a pit, or at any rate, the dead-head was placed below the level at which the metal would flow into it from the furnace. A trough was made from the furnace to the mould, and although there were different ways of accomplishing it, the metal was poured in as quickly as possible. As the metal rose, it was agitated by a pine stick to keep impurities in the center. When the mould was full, charcoal was thrown on top of the sprue to absorb gases and prevent oxidation. The casting was then allowed several days to cool.

When cool, the tube was removed from the mould and the sand cleaned off. It was then ready for boring. This operation was accomplished by supporting the barrel in a horizontal position on a track. Machinery was attached to the square projection of the cascable to give the barrel a rotary motion about its axis. The dead-head was cut off and the bore-cutters were pressed against the revolving face of the muzzle by means of a weight and system of cog-wheels. The cutter was run in until it had completed its job — often in several stages. If a chamber was necessary, this was then done with a smaller cutter, or "chamber-cutter." Some

manufacturers also applied cutting tools to the exterior of the barrel, to shape it to proper size as it turned. The bore was then finished to proper size by a reamer. Except for the trunnions, a planing machine and hand chisels completed the exterior finishing.

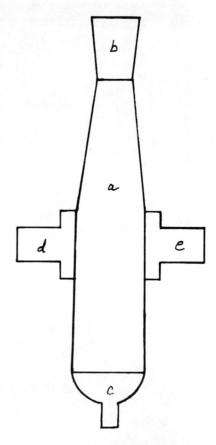

Gregory M. Breneman

Wooden model for the manufacture of cannon.
    a. body
    b. dead-head
    c. breech
    d. trunnion
    e. trunnion

The barrel was then placed in the trunnion lathe. Cutters were pressed against the trunnion faces as the barrel rotated around the trunion axes. Sometimes both trunnions were turned and finished at the same time. The vent was then bored, but the projection on the cascable was not removed until after inspection — this allowed the founder to replace the piece in the machinery to correct any irregularities in the form. If the piece was a smoothbore, inspection followed. If a rifle, it was next rifled.

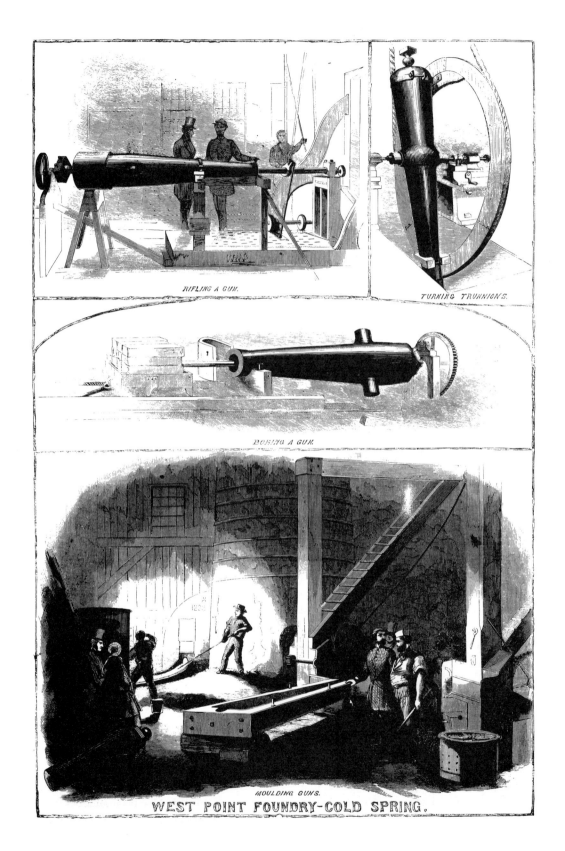

RIFLING A GUN.

TURNING TRUNNIONS.

BORING A GUN.

MOULDING GUNS.

WEST POINT FOUNDRY-COLD SPRING.

Cannon barrel manufacture at the West Point Foundry, Cold Spring, N.Y., as illustrated in the Sept. 14, 1861, issue of "Harpers Weekly." (Bottom) A portion of a mould and flask are show in the center. The trough from the furnace to the gun-pit is in the left center. (Center) The boring of the barrel. (Upper right) The trunnion-turning operation. (Upper left) Rifling a Parrott tube.

Flask and mould for a cannon barrel.

For inspection the tube was placed on skids so that it could be easily moved, and it was carefully examined for flaws and cracks on the exterior and interior, quality of the metal (as far as practicable), and correct dimensions. If it passed inspection, the projection on the cascable was removed and the barrel was ready to be proved.

According to regulations, all barrels were required to be weighed and marked as follows:

1) the number of the gun and the initials of the inspector's name on the face of the muzzle (the numbers in a separate series for each kind and caliber of gun at each factory).
2) the initial letters of the name of the founder, and of the foundry, on the end of the right trunnion.
3) the year of fabrication on the end of the left trunnion.
4) the foundry number on the end of the right rimbase, above the trunnion.
5) the weight in pounds on the base of the breech.
6) the letters U.S. (or C.S.) on the upper surface of the piece.

When viewing surviving specimens, the reader will soon note that the markings varied among manfacturers, and particularly between those in Federal or Confederate service.

CARRIAGES

Field cannon barrels were mounted on wooden carriages that varied only slightly for the different types of tubes. White oak was considered to be the best wood for such purposes. Every part of the carriage with its iron hardware had a name — a simplified parts list is presented below.

   a. handspike inserted in pointing rings
   b. lunette
   c. trail handle
   d. stock or trail
   e. prolonge attached to prolonge hooks
   f. lock chain
   g. elevating screw
   h. cheek
   i. barrel or tube (6-pounder smoothbore)
   j. trunnion cap
   k. handspike mounted on cheek by ring and hook
   l. sponge/rammer attached below carriage by hook and chain
   m. wheel

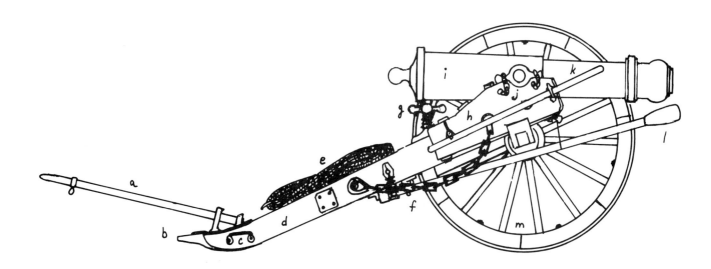

Gregory M. Breneman

For transporting the cannon, the carriage was joined to another two-wheeled vehicle called a limber. This was accomplished by attaching the iron ring (lunette) on the gun carriage trail to an iron pin (pintle) at the rear of the limber and locking them together. The limber carried an ammunition chest that contained fifty rounds of 6-pounder, thirty-two rounds of 12-pounder, or other various quantities of fixed or semi-fixed ammunition depending on the cannons in the battery. In addition, friction primers and fuses were to be found in the chest, and the limber itself was a means of hauling the tar bucket, canvas water buckets, and a large tarpaulin.

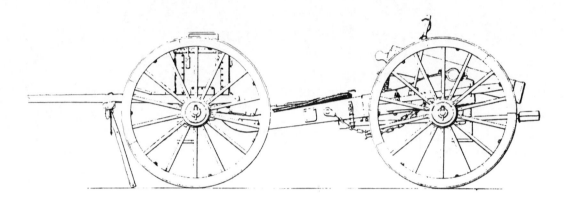

12-pounder howitzer attached to limber

Limber

Additional ammunition was carried in the two ammunition chests on the caisson — a two-wheeled cart attached to its own limber. At least one caisson was assigned to every cannon. The caisson also transported a spare wheel and pole, and some tools.

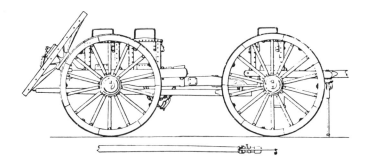

Caisson and limber

Caisson and limber

Equipments and supplies for the battery were carried in the battery wagon. There were over 125 different items, including: carpenter's and saddler's tools, oil, paint, spokes, harness, axes, spades, tarpaulins, spare gunner's implements, and also forage for the horses in the rack on the back.

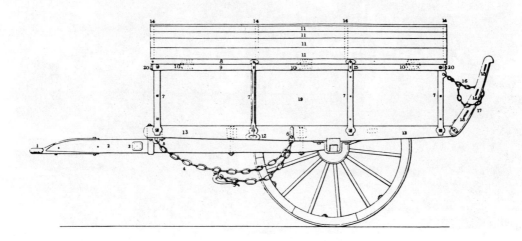

Battery wagon

Iron work repairs and horseshoeing were made possible by the traveling forge attached to each battery. The forge and its limber carried blacksmith's tools, horseshoes, nails, hardware, and other spare items.

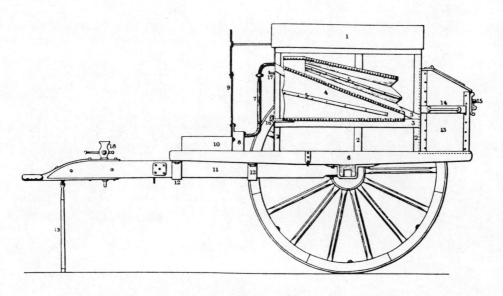

Traveling forge

Making gun carriages at the Watervliet Arsenal, N.Y.

Forging the ironwork for gun carriages at the Watervliet Arsenal, N.Y.

Artillery carriages, limbers, caissons, and other materiel in the Arsenal Yard at the Washington Arsenal, Washington, D.C.

Originally titled "Unfit for Service," this photograph taken on the Gettysburg battlefield in July 1863 shows a disabled limber for a 12-pounder Napoleon with numerous projectiles lying about in the foreground.

TYPES OF PROJECTILES

Four types of regulation projectiles were employed by Civil War field artillery: solid shot, common shell, case shot, and canister. Specimens of 12-pounder "grape shot" exist, but this type of projectile was more often used by siege and heavier weapons in addition to some other less common rounds.

SOLID SHOT — Round (spherical) projectiles of solid iron for smoothbore guns are commonly called "cannonballs" or just plain "shot." When elongated for rifled weapons, the projectile is known as a "bolt." The weight of the solid projectile fired from smoothbore cannons (and some rifled pieces) determined the "pounder" designation. The smashing effect of spherical shot was used against both material objects (opposing batteries, wagons, buildings, etc.) and animate targets. Skilled gunners could ricochet the cannonball across open ground against advancing infantry and cavalry. The conical bolt was not used a great deal by field artillery and was virtually useless for ricochet fire because it tended to bury itself where it first struck the ground (the point of impact). Bolts were anti-materiel, used particularly against masonry fortifications.

COMMON SHELL — The shell, whether spherical or conical, was a hollow iron projectile filled with a black powder bursting charge. It was designed to break into many ragged fragments, although this did not always occur, and was both anti-personnel and anti-materiel. Spherical shells were exploded by time fuses set in wooden or metallic fuse plugs, and were ignited by the flame of the cannon's propelling discharge. Conical shells were detonated by time fuses and impact, or "percussion" fuses. Numerous percussion fuses were invented during the Civil War, generally, all were similar in that they contained a moveable piece called a "slider" and a stationary "anvil." A pistol or musket nipple was attached to the slider and on this was mounted a standard percussion cap. When fired, the slider was held back by inertia, although some fuses did have safety devices. Upon impact, the slider was thrown violently forward, snapping any safety connection, and the percussion cap was crushed and exploded against the anvil. The flame from the percussion cap ingited a small powder train, which in turn communicated with the bursting charge. Percussion fuses had several defects, not the least of which were the slider becoming cocked in some models, or the shell not striking with sufficient force to explode the percussion cap — as in a glancing blow.

Spherical shot strapped to sabot

Solid bolt

Spherical shell

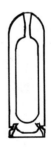

Rifled shell

CASE SHOT — Case shot or "shrapnel" was the invention of Henry Shrapnel, an English artillery officer. It was produced for both smoothbore and rifled weapons. The projectile had a thinner side wall than common shell and was filled with small lead or iron balls in a matrix of sulphur or asphalt. A very small bursting charge was used to merely break open the casing and scatter the contents into the air. In effect, case shot was long-range canister. When the projectile burst and the small balls dispersed, all the parts continued moving forward at a high velocity capable of disabling men and horses. Normally, all case shot was time fused to break open a certain time and distance from the cannon, since the small bursting charge would have had little effect once it struck the ground.

A notable difference between Union and Confederate case shot was the manner in which the chamber was formed for the bursting charge. In the North, the interior of the projectile was entirely filled with lead balls and a sulphur matrix to the bottom of the fuse hole. After the matrix had set up, the chamber was drilled out. Due to a scarcity of lead, Confederate case shot balls were generally of iron which were much more difficult to drill. Southern case shot is usually found with a side filler hole in the casing. A stick or "mandrel" was inserted into the fuse hole and the balls and matrix poured through the side hole into the projectile. When the matrix had hardened, the mandrel was withdrawn, and thus the chamber was formed. The side hole was normally plugged with lead, although specimens are observed with brass and iron screw plugs.

CANISTER — The effect of this round when fired from a cannon was like that of a huge shotgun blast. Canister consisted of a number of large balls, usually of iron, packed with sawdust in a tinned iron cylinder. As an example, the 12-pounder Napoleon canister had twenty-seven 1½-inch-diameter iron balls. The cylinder was nailed to a large wooden plug or "culot" on one end and crimped over a heavy iron plate on the other. Upon discharge, the cylinder disintegrated and the balls fanned out. Canister was extremely effective against attacking infantry and cavalry up to a range of 200 yards, and probably had a maximum range of 400 yards. At very close range, numerous contemporary accounts mentioned the loading of cannons with two and even three rounds of canister, but this was not a safe practice for the gunners.

GRAPE SHOT — Grape shot was similar to canister in effect and range, but differed greatly in the manner of manufacture. A common "stand" of grape consisted of heavy iron top and bottom plates, nine iron balls in three tiers, two iron rings, all held together by a nut and bolt, with a rope carrying handle. An earlier variation was known as "quilted" grape. It had an iron pin or pipe sticking up from the center of the bottom plate and dispensed with the top plate. The balls were piled around the pin and then wrapped in canvas. Heavy twine laced between the balls to keep them rigid gave the appearance of quilting.

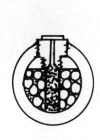
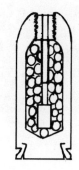

Spherical case shot   Rifled case shot

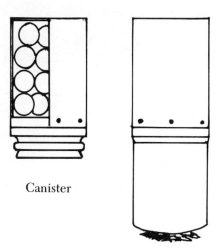

Canister

"Fixed" round of canister ammunition

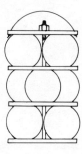

Stand of grapeshot

Various sizes of lead (white) and iron case shot and canister balls.

Contents of a fired 12-pounder canister — 27 1.5" iron balls with plates.

Stands of "quilted" grape scattered around the remains of a cannon destroyed by the Confederates upon their evacuation of the Yorktown, Va., defenses, 1862.

18

Filling spherical case shot with the sulphur matrix at the Watervliet Arsenal, N.Y.

Strapping spherical case shot to the wooden sabot at the Watervliet Arsenal, N.Y.

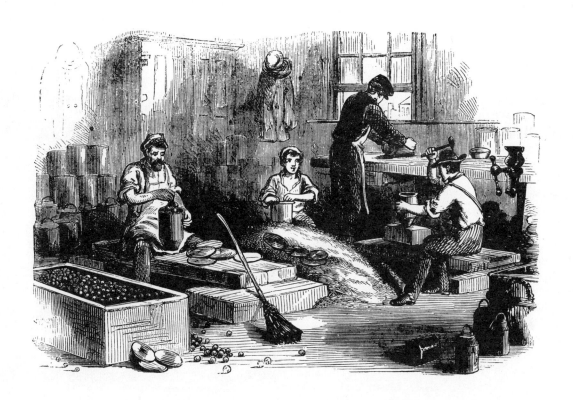

Filling canister at the Watervliet Arsenal, N.Y.

Spherical projectiles for smoothbores were attached to a wooden cup or "sabot" by tinned iron straps. A groove in the base of the sabot allowed the powder bag to be tied to it. This complete round was known as "fixed" ammunition. When the powder bag was loaded separately from the saboted ball (or rifled projectile), this was called "semi-fixed." The sabot and straps served to keep the fuses of explosive projectiles pointed toward the muzzle. Otherwise, without the sabot, the ball could be loaded with the fuse against the powder charge — a dangerous condition that could have resulted in the fuse being driven into the projectile and exploding it prematurely in the tube.

For muzzleloading rifled weapons to be effective, whether small-arm or cannon, the projectile had to be expanded to engage the rifling. Inventors of the Civil War-era artillery ammunition accomplished this in numerous ways that generally fall into one of three basic systems:

A. Expansion cup

Attached to the base of the projectile body was a metal cup, ring, or disc of softer metal also called a "sabot." When loaded, this cup was of the same diameter as the rest of the projectile, but when fired, the gases from the powder charge expanded the cup into the lands and grooves of the rifle. The following are examples of this system:

Parrott — wrought iron ring
Reed — copper ring
Burton — lead cup
Mullane — copper disc

B. Forcing cone

The rear portion of the projectile body was tapered toward the base and was fitted with a ring of lead or other material. When fired, the ring was expanded by being forced up the cone, either by the propelling gases or other aids. The following are examples of this system:

Archer — lead ring
Schenkl — papier-maché
Hotchkiss — lead ring and iron cup

C. Pre-guided flight

The projectile was of the same shape as the bore of the rifle, but slightly smaller in diameter, or was otherwise directed to take a predetermined path by studs or flanges. The Whitworth and other projectiles of British origin are examples of this system.

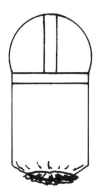

"Fixed" round of solid-shot amunition

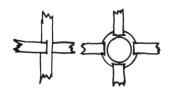

Strap arrangements for spherical shot and fused ball

All line drawings in this section by Gregory M. Breneman.

Assorted artillery projectiles, including various stands of grape, at the ruins of the Arsenal, Richmond, Va., 1865.

20

MANUFACTURE OF PROJECTILES

The moulds used for casting projectiles were similar to those used in the manufacture of cannon barrels. The models, however, at least for spherical shot and shell, consisted of copper hemispheres which fitted together by a tongue and groove to form a perfect sphere. Each hemisphere had a threaded hole in the bottom into which a handle could be attached from the inside or outside. The flask for the mould was a sheet-iron box with an open top and bottom that was separable into halves.

To build the mould, the hemisphere with the groove was placed on a flat board and a handle screwed into the threaded hole. One half of the flask was positioned on the board with the hemisphere in the center. A round stick for forming the casting channel was held in its proper position to the side of the hemisphere. Moulding sand was then firmly packed around the three parts until the flask was full (see drawing A). The sand was accurately leveled, the handle and stick removed, and a bottom attached to the flask.

This half was carefully turned over and the second hemisphere attached to the first. The handle was screwed into the threaded hole and the remaining half of the flask adjusted on top. Dry sand was sprinkled on the half-mould formed, to prevent the other from sticking to it. Moulding sand was again firmly packed in until the flask was full (see drawing B). The sand was leveled, the handle removed, and the bottom attached like before.

The top half of the flask was taken off and turned over, and the two hemispheres were removed by screwing in the handle to the inside and carefully lifting them out. A passage was cut across from the channel to the interior of the mould and any needed repairs were made by hand. If solid shot was to be cast, the hole in the bottom of the second half formed was closed with sand. Both halves of the mould were coated with coke-wash and baked in the oven until thoroughly dried. When cool, the halves were joined with the channel opening facing upwards.

CASTING SHOT — With the hole at the bottom closed, the mould was ready for casting shot. The molten iron was brought from the furnace to the mould in a ladle or bucket and poured into the casting channel. The metal entering from the side prevented injury to the form. The opening in the top allowed for the escape of gas, served as a collecting area for any impurities, and furnished metal to supply the shrinkage caused by cooling (see drawing C).

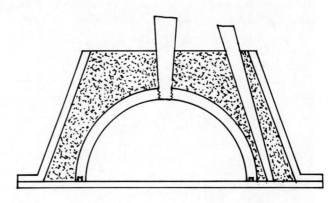

Gregory M. Breneman

A. First half of mould and flask for spherical ball.

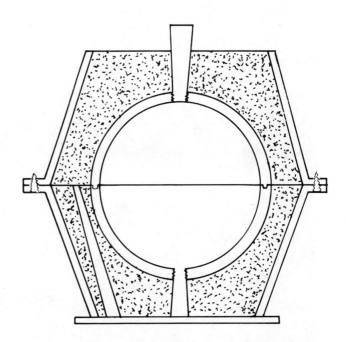

Gregory M. Breneman

B. Completed mould and flask for spherical ball. Neither of the copper hemispheres has been removed, nor has the casting channel been cut.

Confederate artillery ammunition, torpedoes, and other paraphernalia collected at the Charleston Arsenal, Charleston, S.C., after its re-occupation by Federal forces in 1865.

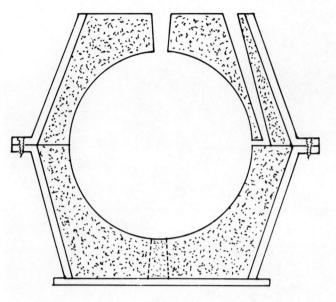

C. Mould and flask for casting a spherical shot.

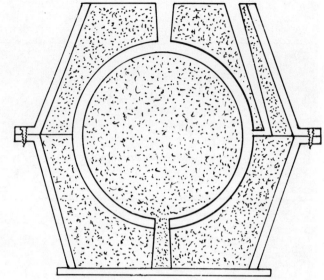

D. Mould and flask for casting a spherical shell.

CASTING SHELL — The mould for casting a shell was made as above, but required a core to produce the hollow center. The core was a sphere of refractory sand compressed by two cups on to a heavy wire stem. In turn, the stem was covered to the proper size with the moulding composition. The stem not only supported the core, but also formed the fuse opening. The stem was placed into the hole at the bottom of the mould, which for shot was closed. By means of a gauge, the core was positioned exactly in the center of the mould. Failure to do so would have resulted in uneven wall thicknesses. Molten iron was poured into the channel as when casting shot, and gas escaped through the hole in the top of the mould. When the casting was cool, the core of sand was broken up and removed (see drawing D).

After casting, the excess metal had to be removed from both shot and shell with a hammer and chisel. This excess was to be found at the channel, dead-head, and where the mould halves joined (the mould line). A number of the balls were then placed in a large revolving iron cylinder, where by friction of rubbing against each other, they were polished to a more uniform surface.

The projectiles, like cannon, had to pass inspection. They were checked visually for any noticeable flaws. Gauges and other means ascertained their correct diameter, wall thickness, strength, and weight. Those that passed were coated with lacquer and placed in piles until they were wanted.

Stockpiles of artillery ammunition at the Washington Arsenal, Washington, D.C.

Federal "Ordnance Yard," Morris Island, S.C., November 1864. The wooden boxes in the foreground each contained one large-caliber, rifled artillery projectile.

24

FRICTION PRIMERS and TIME FUSES

The friction primer was the principal means of igniting the powder charge in the cannons of both North and South. Basically, it consisted of two copper tubes (the Confederates experimented with pewter and even paper) soldered together at right angles. The short tube was filled with a friction composition into which was inserted a wire serrated on the end. The other end of the wire was twisted to form a loop. Musket powder filled the long tube, which was closed with a plug of wax. The primer was then varnished to make it somewhat waterproof.

To fire the cannon, the long shaft of the friction primer was placed into the vent and the wire loop bent so that it was horizontal. The hook of the lanyard was attached to the loop and at the appropriate time was given a pull. The serrated wire drawing through the friction composition ignited it and in turn the musket powder, the flame communicating quickly with the powder charge in the bore.

Package of five friction primers made at the Frankford Arsenal, Philadelphia, Pa.

Friction primers

Package of twelve friction primers made at the Richmond Arsenal, Va., C.S.

The paper time fuse consisted of a paper cylinder packed with black powder whose rate of burning at a given pressure was supposedly known. Graduations in seconds on the outside of the paper case enabled the gunner to shorten the fuse if a decreased burning time was desire to burst the projectile. To secure uniformity in their fuses, the Federal Ordnance Department, in October 1862, directed that all paper time fuses were to be made at the Frankford Arsenal. Confederate time fuses were made at a number of ordnance establishments and seem to have always varied in quality and rate of burning.

Paper time fuses were inserted in wooden or metallic fuse plugs and were ignited by the gases of the propelling charge. In the North, they were replaced for the most part in spherical projectiles by the Bormann time fuse; however, in elongated case shot projectiles, their use continued. Confederates used the paper time fuse throughout the war in spherical and elongated shells and case shot.

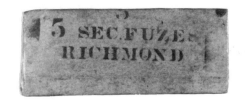

Packages of 2- and 5-second time fuses, Richmond Arsenal.

8-second time fuse   Wooden fuse plug   Assorted Confederate time fuses

Package of 5-second fuses, Frankford Arsenal   Bormann time fuse   C.S. copper fuse plugs

6-POUNDER FIELD GUN (BRONZE), MODEL 1841

This smoothbore weapon was one of the models of 6-pounder field guns that were used by both Union and Confederate forces, at least during the early stages of the Civil War. Owing to advances made in the 1850s, the 6-pounder was virtually obsolete by 1861. Necessity dictated that they be pressed into service; however, battlefield experience further demonstrated their inadequacy and the growing numbers of Napoleons and 3-inch rifles led to the 6-pounder's demise. In the C. S. service, bronze 6-pounders were ordered to be melted down for other weapons, and in the North, many were rifled into the James System of 15 lands and grooves. At the Battle of Gettysburg in July 1863, only one 6-pounder was on the field, and that was in Latham's North Carolina Battery, a part of Longstreet's Corps, A. N. V. Many 6-pounders that now dot our National Military Parks have been altered to make them appear as if they were 12-pounder Napoleons. The first few inches of the bore were enlarged and external moldings were removed. This was done, due to a shortage of 12-pounder Napoleons to mark actual battery locations.

6-pounder field gun

Bore Diameter . . . . 3.67"
Tube Material . . . . Bronze
Length of Tube . . . . 60"
Weight of Tube . . . . 884 lbs.
Powder Charge . . . . 1.25 lbs.
Range at 5° Elevation . . . . 1,523 yards

6-pounder shot attached to sabot
Weight — 6 lbs.
Diameter — 3.58"

6-pounder shell, Bormann fuse
Weight — 4 lbs.
Diameter — 3.58"

6-pounder canister
Weight — 12.5 lbs.
Diameter — 3.58"
Length — 6.75"

12-POUNDER FIELD GUN, MODEL 1857
(The Napoleon)

This smoothbore weapon was developed in France in the 1850s and was named for Emperor Napoleon III. It was designed to fire shot, shell, case shot, and canister. The Napoleon has been termed the "workhorse" of Civil War artillery, for its maneuverability and overall effectiveness both at long-range dueling and in close against onrushing infantry, it had no peer. Confederate General Robert E. Lee was impressed with its worth. On December 5, 1862, he wrote to the Secretary of War:

> . . . The best guns for field service, in my opinion, are the 12-pounder Napoleons, the 10-pounder Parrotts, and the approved 3-inch rifles. . . . The contest between our 6-pounder smoothbores and the 12-pounder Napoleons of the enemy is very unequal, and in addition, is discouraging to our artillerists. . . .

In July 1863, an interesting statistic reveals that Napoleons comprised 39 percent of the artillery armament of both the Union Army of the Potomac and the Confederate Army of Northern Virginia: U. S. — 142 out of 360, and C. S. — 107 out of 272.

Napoleons were produced by both North and South. Generally, they are distinguished by the Federal Napoleons having a muzzle swell and the Confederate version merely a straight tube.

12-pounder field gun — Napoleon, Federal manufacture

Bore Diameter . . . . 4.62"
Tube Material . . . . Bronze
Length of Tube . . . . 66"
Weight of Tube . . . . 1,227 lbs.
Powder Charge . . . . 2.5 lbs.
Range at 5° Elevation . . . . 1,619 yards

12-pounder field gun — Napoleon, Confederate manufacture

12-pounder shot
Weight — 12 lbs.
Diameter — 4.52"

12-pounder shell, Bormann time fuse
Weight — 8 lbs.
Diameter — 4.52"

12-pounder shell, C.S., wooden fuse plug
Weight — 8.5 lbs.
Diameter — 4.52"

Federal ammunition shipping crate for eight 12-pounder shells.

12-pounder case, C.S., copper fuse plug (left to right): lead, copper, and iron side plugs.
Weight — 10 lbs.
Diameter — 4.52"

A Federal battery of six 12-pounder Napoleons near Falmouth, opposite Fredericksburg, Va., 1863.

Confederate artillery (12-pounder Napoleons) captured at Missionary Ridge near Chattanooga, Tenn., November 1863.

FIELD HOWITZERS

As mentioned earlier, the howitzer was a short-barreled cannon designed to throw large projectiles with a relatively small powder charge concentrated in a chamber in its breech. It fired the same projectiles as a gun of similar caliber, but did so at a higher trajectory.

The 12-pounder Napoleon virtually replaced all 12-pounder howitzers in the Federal service; however, due to a serviceable weapon need on the Confederate side, it was slower to disappear there. Lee hauled 26 12-pounder field howitzers to Gettysburg.

	12-pdr.	*24-pdr.*
Bore Diameter	4.62"	5.82"
Tube Material	Bronze	Bronze
Length of Tube	53"	65"
Weight of Tube	788 lbs.	1,318 lbs.
Powder Charge	1 lb.	2 lbs.
Range at 5° Elevation	1,072 yards	1,322 yards

12-pounder field howitzer, Confederate manufacture

24-pounder field howitzer, Austrian manufacture, imported by the South.

24-pounder shot
Weight — 24 lbs.
Diameter — 5.68"

24-pounder shell, Bormann fuse
Weight — 17 lbs.
Diameter — 5.68"

12-POUNDER MOUNTAIN HOWITZER

The 12-pounder mountain howitzer probably saw more use in the Mexican War and on the Western prairie than it did during the Civil War, but its unique features are at least worthy of mention. Although a smoothbore with the same bore diameter as the Napoleon and capable of firing the same projectiles, it was small enough to be completely broken down and transported on pack animals. Ammunition and other equipment were packed in the same way. For field use it did not employ a limber, but was moved by a lone animal attached to the trail by two poles.

Bore Diameter .... 4.62”
Tube Material .... Bronze
Length of Tube .... 37”
Weight of Tube .... 220 lbs.
Powder Charge .... .5 lb.
Range at 5° Elevation .... 900 yards

12-pounder howitzer canister, probably C.S.
Weight — 9 lbs.
Diameter — 4.5”
Length — 6.4”

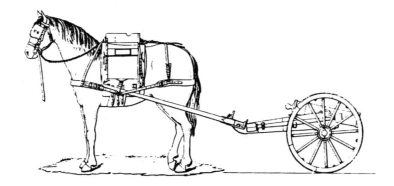

12-pounder mountain howiter: (top) limbered to be drawn by one animal; (bottom) broken down and packed — tube (left), carriage (center), and ammunition (right).

PARROTT FIELD RIFLES, 10-POUNDER AND 20-POUNDER

The Parrott rifles were patented in 1861, by Robert P. Parrott and cast by him as superintendent of the West Point Foundry, Cold Spring, New York. While not the best rifles to be put into service, they were available, inexpensive, and accurate. The Confederates even went so far as to produce their own copies.

The Parrotts are easily identified by the wrought iron reinforcing band around the breech. Although not all banded cannons are Parrotts, the Parrotts are by far the most commonly encountered. Parrott's band was made by winding a bar of iron around a form or mandrel and then hammering it until welded solid. What Parrott claimed as new was his method of attaching the band. While hot, the band was forced onto the breech of the horizontally rotating tube that was being water-cooled on the inside. The band greatly increased the strength of the breech, but many Parrott rifles burst in front of this juncture.

Often a term of confusion, the "pounder" designation does not always accurately describe Parrott rifles. The 10-pounder, Model 1861, has a bore diameter of 2.9 inches while the 10-pounder, Model 1863, has a 3.0-inch bore. Ammunition specifically made for the latter model could not be used in the Model 1861; however, the reverse situation was possible. The two guns are readily identified by the lack of a muzzle swell on the Model 1863. Additionally, some larger Parrott rifles were known by totally different "pounder" designations in the Army and in the Navy.

A solid iron bolt was produced to be fired by Parrott field rifles; however, the most common ammunition used was shell and case. Canister was always to be found in the chests, but when fired from the rifles it was not as effective as when fired from a howitzer or Napoleon. The rifled barrel tended to throw the canister balls into an erratic, spiralled pattern.

10-pounder Parrott field rifle, Model 1861

10-pounder Parrott field rifle, Model 1863

	10-pdr.	20-pdr.
Bore Diameter, M61, 2.9"; M63, 3.0"		3.67"
Tube Material	Iron	Iron
Length of Tube	78"	89"
Weight of Tube	890 lbs.	1,750 lbs.
Powder Charge	1 lb.	2 lbs.
Range at 5° Elevation	2,000 yards	2,100 yards

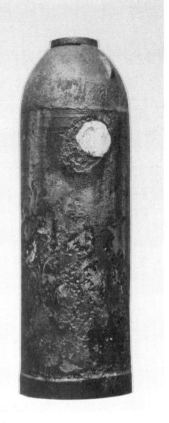

10-pounder Parrott shell, U.S.,
zinc fuse plug
  Weight — 9 lbs.
  Diameter — 2.88"
  Length — 8.5"

10-pounder Parrott case, U.S.,
rare, with Bormann time fuse
  Weight — 11.5 lbs.
  Diameter — 2.88"
  Length — 8.5"

10-pounder Parrott case, C.S.,
copper fuse plug, lead side plug
  Weight — 10.5 lbs.
  Diameter — 2.88"
  Length — 8.625"

**Metallic fuse plugs for Parrott projectiles. The specimen at right is Confederate and made of copper. The other four are
Federal and made of zinc.**

20-pounder Parrott case, U.S., short variety
Weight — 20 lbs.
Diameter — 3.63"
Length — 9.25"

20-pounder Parrott shell, U.S., long variety
Weight — 17 lbs.
Diameter — 3.63"
Length — 10.375"

Federal ammunition shipping crate for ten 20-pounder shells.

20-pounder Parrott field rifle, Confederate manufacture

20-pounder Parrott shell, C.S., short variety; chipping at base occurred when shell was fired
    Weight — 18 lbs.
    Diameter — 3.63"
    Length — 9.5"

20-pounder Parrott shell, C.S., long variety, iron sabot
    Weight — 16 lbs.
    Diameter — 3.63"
    Length — 10"

20-pounder Parrott shell, C.S., long variety, copper sabot
    Weight — 18 lbs.
    Diameter — 3.63"
    Length — 10"

Four 20-pounder Parrott field rifles of the 1st New York artillery on the "Peninsula" near Richmond, Va., June 1862.

Federal gun crew drilling with a 20-pounder Parrott field rifle.

Confederate-made projectiles for 3-inch rifles:

Archer bolt
  Weight — 8.3 lbs.
  Diameter — 2.94"
  Length — 5.75"

Burton shell
  Weight — 8 lbs.
  Diameter — 2.94"
  Length — 7.4"

Burton case
  Weight — 10.2 lbs.
  Diameter — 2.94"
  Length — 7"

Reed-Broun shell
  Weight — 9 lbs.
  Diameter — 2.94"
  Length — 7.5"

Mullane shell (short)
  Weight — 6 lbs.
  Diameter — 2.94"
  Length — 6"

Mullane shell
  Weight — 7 lbs.
  Diameter — 2.94"
  Length — 8"

Reed shell
  Weight — 7.4 lbs.
  Diameter — 2.94"
  Length — 7.5"

Reed case
  Weight — 10.4 lbs.
  Diameter — 2.88"
  Length — 7.75"

3-INCH ORDNANCE RIFLE

The 3-inch Ordnance Rifle was developed by one John Griffen, who secured a patent for it in 1855. Most of these weapons were produced by the Phoenix Iron Company of Phoenixville, Pa. The president of Phoenix, Samuel J. Reeves, made improvements to the wrought iron forging and welding process and was issued his own patent in 1862.

Tests with four experimental wrought iron cannons in early 1861 led to their adoption by the Federal Ordnance Department. The Ordnance Rifle is distinctive with its sleek lines and lack of external decoration. Over 1,000 were purchased by the North. These weapons were sturdy, accurate, and superior to the 10-pounder Parrott. At Gettysburg, 146 or 41 percent of Meade's 360 guns were 3-inch Ordnance Rifles. Many captured guns with their projectiles were used by the South.

The 3-inch Ordnance Rifle usually fired Hotchkiss or Schenkl patented shells or case shot. It could shoot 10-pounder Parrott ammunition in a pinch, and like the Parrott it was less effective with canister than a smoothbore.

Bore Diameter	3.0"
Tube Material	Wrought Iron
Length of Tube	73"
Weight of Tube	816 lbs.
Powder Charge	1 lb.
Range at 5° Elevation	1,835 yards

3-inch Hotchkiss shell, percussion fuse
Weight — 8 lbs.
Diameter — 2.88"
Length — 6.5"

3-inch Hotchkiss case, time fuse
Weight — 9 lbs.
Diameter — 2.88"
Length — 6.75"

3-inch Ordnance rifle

Two different Hotchkiss time fuse plugs made of brass.

Shipping crate for ten 3-inch Hotchkiss canisters.

3-inch Hotchkiss canister, side view and enlargement of lead base
     Weight — 6 lbs.
     Diameter — 2.9"
     Length — 8"

3-inch Schenkl shell with brass percussion fuse
     Weight — 8 lbs.
     Diameter — 2.94"
     Length — 9"

3-inch Schenkl case, zinc combination time/percussion fuse, papier-maché sabot intact
     Weight — 9 lbs.
     Diameter — 2.94"
     Length — 9"

A Federal battery of six 3-inch Ordnance rifles limbered and in marching order, photographed near Fair Oaks, Va., June 1862.

3-inch Ordnance rifles of Cooper's Battery "B," 1st Pennsylvania Light Artillery before Petersburg, Va., June 1864.

14-POUNDER (3.8-inch) JAMES RIFLE

This weapon was developed by Rhode Island militia General Charles T. James, presumably to fire rifled projectiles of his invention. Although of dissimilar material, it is very close in outward appearance to the 3-inch Ordnance Rifle. These guns were produced by the Ames Manufacturing Company, Chicopee, Mass., in 1861 and 1862. By the time of the inventor's death in October 1862, James' projectiles were not highly regarded and other ammunition was substituted so long as the rifles remained in service.

14-pounder James rifle

Bore Diameter	3.80"
Tube Material	Bronze
Length of Tube	65"
Weight of Tube	918 lbs.
Powder Charge	.75 lb.
Range at 5° Elevation	1,700 yards

3.8-inch James pattern II shell
Weight — 16.5 lbs.
Diameter — 3.75"
Length — 7.75"

3.8-inch Hotchkiss case (for James rifle)
Weight — 14 lbs.
Diameter — 3.73"
Length — 7.25"

12-POUNDER (2.75-inch) WHITWORTH BREECHLOADING RIFLE

The 2.75-inch Whitworth Breechloading Rifle was developed in England by Sir Joseph Whitworth before the American Civil War and was one of several types of Whitworth cannons imported into this country during the conflict. Whitworths are generally associated with Confederate usage; however, one battery of 2.75-inch rifles was in Federal service from 1861 until the close of the war. Surprisingly, this battery saw little field service except during the Peninsula Campaign of 1862, and then remained in the defenses of Washington, D.C.

In a paper written in 1866, Confederate General E. P. Alexander, chief of artillery of James Longstreet's Corps, had the following to say about the Whitworth:

> One muzzle-loading six-pounder and six breechloading twelve-pounder Whitworths were distributed through the army and often rendered valuable service by their great range and accuracy. They fired solid shot almost exclusively; but they were perfectly reliable and their projectiles never failed to fly in the most beautiful trajectory imaginable. Their breechloading arrangements, however, often worked with difficulty and every one of the six was at sometime disabled by the breaking of some of its parts but all were repaired again and kept in service. As a general field-piece, its efficiency was impaired by its weight and the very cumbrous English carriage on which it was mounted and while a few with an army may often be valuable, the United States three-inch rifle is much more generally servicable with good ammunition.

Sir Joseph Whitworth was a prolific inventor of cannons, small arms, projectiles for both, and machinery for producing all of the aforementioned. His weapons had a unique bore design — being in the shape of a hexagon. The cannon projectiles are of this same shape, but are of an ever-so-slightly smaller diameter. Not rifled in the normal sense, the twisted hexagonal bore presented a path for the projectile to follow. This gave the Whitworth its extreme range and accuracy. At 35° elevation, the 2.75-inch rifle could throw a projectile 10,000 yards or 5.7 miles, but it is very doubtful if it was ever employed in combat at this distance due to a need to see the target.

As alluded to by Alexander, the breechloading design had its drawbacks, and the rifle was not necessarily more quickly loaded than a muzzleloader. But if the breechloading mechanism was in disrepair, the Whitworth could be loaded from the muzzle.

Also as reported by Alexander, the Whitworth was more often used with solid iron bolts — the explosive shell held little powder to be really effective. The projectile in flight was said by Union troops to make a very eerie sound. When loaded with English-made ammunition, the powder charge was encased in a tin cylinder also of hexagonal shape.

Bore Diameter . . . . 2.75"
Tube Material . . . . Iron & Steel
Length of Tube . . . . 104"
Weight of Tube . . . . 1,092 lbs.
Powder Charge . . . . 1.75 lbs.
Range at 5° Elevation . . . . 2,800 yards

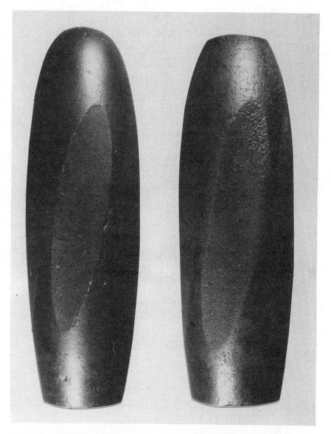

2.75-inch Whitworth bolt
   Weight — 12.75 lbs.
   Diameter — 2.75"
   Length — 8.875"

2.75-inch Whitworth shell
   Weight — 9.75 lbs.
   Diameter — 2.75"
   Length — 8.75"

2.75-inch Whitworth breechloading rifle photographed at Richmond, Va., April 1865.

30-POUNDER PARROTT RIFLE

The 30-pounder or 4.2-inch Parrott rifle was the next progression in the Parrott line after then 10- and 20-pounder field pieces and was employed in several theatres with good success. Technicallly a siege and garrison weapon, it was usually mounted on a wooden siege carriage for use where operations slowed and it could be brought to bear from somewhat prepared positions; however, the 30-pounder Parrott captured by the Confederates at the First Battle of Bull Run was mounted on a field carriage. Percussion shells were typically fired from these weapons, but case shot and bolts were also available.

Bore Diameter	4.2"
Tube Material	Iron
Length of Tube	133"
Weight of Tube	4,200 lbs.
Powder Charge	3.75 lbs.
Range at 5° Elevation	2,200 yards

MOLLUS

30-pounder Parrott rifle in Battery Hays against Fort Wagner, Morris Island, S.C.

National Archives

Three 30-pounder Parrott rifles of Burton's Co. "I," 1st Connecticut Heavy Artillery, Petersburg, Va., June 1864.

45

4.5-INCH SIEGE RIFLE, MODEL 1861

This weapon is similar in appearance to the smaller 3-inch Ordnance Rifle and is often called the 4.5-inch Ordnance Rifle, but unlike its cousin was produced from cast iron — not wrought iron. Two batteries accompanied the Army of the Potomac from Fredericksburg to the final crossing of the Rapidan River; however, during the Gettysburg campaign they got no closer to the battlefield than Westminster, Md. Contemporary writers praised the weapon for its accuracy, range, and even though mounted on the siege carriage, its mobility. It usually fired Hotchkiss or Schenkl patent projectiles that weighed about 30 pounds.

Bore Diameter .... 4.5"
Tube Material .... Iron
Length of Tube .... 133"
Weight of Tube .... 3,450 lbs.
Powder Charge .... 3.5 lbs.
Range at 5° Elevation .... 2,100 yards

4.5-inch siege rifles in position at Falmouth, Va., but limbered for travel. Fredericksburg is in the background.

24-POUNDER COEHORN MORTAR

This weapon was named for the Dutchman, Baron van Menno Coehoorn, who invented it in the late 1600s. The tube of the U. S. Model of 1838 was cast of bronze and was mounted on a wooden bed with four handles. Although two men could maneuver its almost 300 total pounds, it was ideally served by a four-man crew.

The Confederates used captured Coehorns and also produced some of their own in both 24-pounder and 12-pounder sizes. The tubes for these weapons were of cast iron. While the North used standard 24-pounder shells in their Coehorns, the South developed special projectiles with "ears" cast into the shell body near the fuse hole. These were loaded by shell hooks like the larger mortar balls and ensured that the fuse pointed away from the powder charge to prevent premature explosions.

Eight Coehorns accompanied the Union Army of the Potomac when it began its southward march in May 1864. They were well suited to lobbing shells short distances in the trench warfare that developed and saw extensive use during the siege of Petersburg.

"General Grant's campaign — shelling the enemy from the Coehorns." Sketched by A. R. Waud, this drawing originally appeared in the July 30, 1864, issue of *Harper's Weekly*.

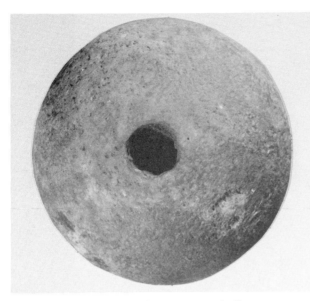

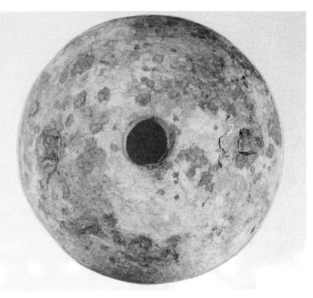

24-pounder Coehorn mortar shell, U.S.
Weight — 17 lbs.
Diameter — 5.68"

24-pounder Coehorn mortar shell, C.S.; "ears" are seen
at 3 and 9 o'clock
Weight — 17 lbs.
Diameter — 5.68"

Ordnance captured after the fall of Richmond, Va., April 1865. Of special note are the two 24-pounder, Confederate, iron Coehorn mortars — one is in the foreground and the other is at the extreme right. The beds are merely large blocks of solid wood with handles attached. Three standard Federal bronze Coehorns are in the center of the photograph in front of the long row of cannons. The large mortar is an 8-inch siege & garrison, Model 1841. The weapon on the broken carriage is a 32-pounder smoothbore, Model 1846. Cannons in the background are Parrott field rifles and three 8-inch siege howitzers.

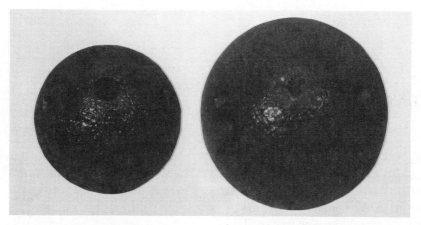

8-inch mortar shell	10-inch mortar shell
Weight — 44 lbs.	Weight — 88 lbs.
Diameter — 7.88"	Diameter — 9.87"

	24-pounder Coehorn	*8-inch Siege*	*10-inch Siege*	*10-inch Seacoast*	*13-inch Seacoast*
Bore Diameter	5.82"	8.0"	10.0"	10.0"	13.0"
Tube Material	Bronze	Iron	Iron	Iron	Iron
Length of Tube	16.32"	22.5"	28"	46"	53"
Weight of Tube	164 lbs.	930 lbs.	1,852 lbs.	5,775 lbs.	17,120 lbs.
Powder Charge	.5 lb.	3.75 lbs.	4.0 lbs.	10.0 lbs.	20.0 lbs.
Range at 45° Elevation	1,200 yds.	1,200 yds.	2,100 yds.	4,250 yds.	4,325 yds.

Mounting 10-inch seacoast mortars near Butler's Crow's Nest, Va., 1864.

13-INCH SEACOAST MORTAR, MODEL 1861

The 13-inch Seacoast Mortar probably saw little, if any, use by the Confederates, but was put in action by Union troops at several locations during the war. This cast iron monster was supported by an iron bed and could throw its 200-pound shell almost 2½ miles. The now-famous "Dictator" was a mortar of this type and the only one deployed by the Federals in the Petersburg lines. It remained in use for only about three months before being sent to the rear. The 8-inch and 10-inch mortars had been found to be more effective.

As mentioned earlier, the 8-, 10-, and 13-inch mortar balls were cast with "ears" on either side of the fuse opening. At least two men with shell hooks were required to load the ball into the tube. Because of the high trajectory and length of time to the target, mortar fuses were much longer than those used in other shells. The wooden plug fit well down into the bursting charge.

Wooden fuse plug for large mortar shells.

13-inch seacoast mortars in Battery No. 4 near Yorktown, Va., 1862. Note the rachet for elevating the tube.

The 13-inch mortar "The Dictator" in its first position on a specially built railroad flatcar, Petersburg, Va., 1864.

"The Dictator" in its final position at Petersburg to the rear of captured Confederate Battery 5. Note the shell hooks in the "ears" of the ball on top of the pile at right.

32-POUNDER SEACOAST GUN

In the scheme of things during the Civil War, the 32-pounder Seacoast gun was used extensively in land fortifications guarding major cities. They were photographed quite often in some of the forts surrounding Washington, D.C., and are usually seen mounted on wooden, front pintle, barbette carriages. An interesting feature of the Model 1829 is the breeching loop on the knob of the cascable for Naval use. A 42-pounder, Model of 1831, is a companion piece. This smoothbore was made of cast iron and employed the full range of ammunition: shot, shell, case, canister, and grape. Those captured and in Confederate positions probably saw more battle use than any in Federal service.

	32-pdr.	42-pdr.
Bore Diameter	6.4"	7.0"
Tube Material	Iron	Iron
Length of Tube	125"	129"
Weight of Tube	7,200 lbs.	8,500 lbs.
Powder Charge	8 lbs.	10.5 lbs.
Range at 5° Elevation	1,922 yards	1,955 yards

National Archives

View of Fort Stevens, part of the defenses of Washington, D.C., showing three 32-pounder, iron seacoast guns, Model 1829, mounted on wooden, front pintle, barbette carriages. The artillerymen are variously serving their pieces for this staged photograph.

PARROTT HEAVY RIFLES, SEACOAST

The 100-pounder (6.4-inch), the 200-pounder (8-inch), and the 300-pounder (10-inch) were the largest Parrott rifles produced at the West Point Foundry. On land, the 100-pounder was mounted on an iron carriage in seacoast fortifications, or in prepared siege positions. The Navy used quite a few 6.4- and 8-inch Parrotts at sea, but all three sizes had a bad habit of bursting. The famous "Swamp Angel" in the Marsh Battery behind Morris Island, S. C., was an 8-inch rifle that burst at its 36th round.

	6.4-inch	8-inch	10-inch
Bore Diameter	6.4"	8.0"	10.0"
Tube Material	Iron	Iron	Iron
Length of Tube	151"	159"	173"
Weight of Tube	9,700 lbs.	16,300 lbs.	26,500 lbs.
Weight of Projectile	100 lbs.	175 lbs.	250 lbs.
Powder Charge	10 lbs.	16 lbs.	25 lbs.
Range at 5° Elevation	Maximum ranges in excess of 8,000 yards, although the 10-inch was not tried.		

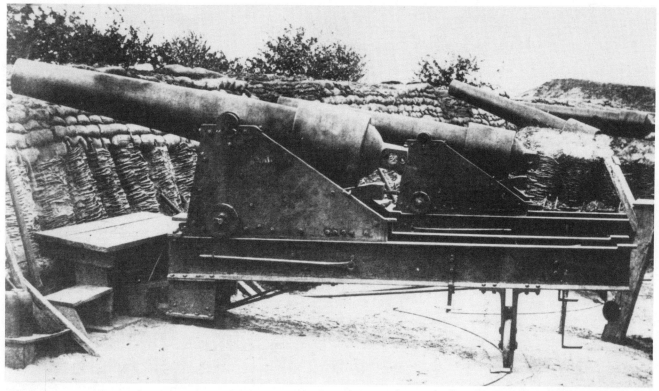

National Archives

Battery No. 1 before Yorktown, Va., 1862 — 100-pounder (6.4-inch) Parrott rifles mounted on wrought iron, front pintle, barbette carriages. Note the quoins for elevating the tubes.

April 1865 view of the Confederate Battery Dantzler on the James River below Richmond, Va. The cannon is a C.S.-manufactured answer to the Parrott heavy rifle — a double-banded Brooke seacoast rifle, mounted on a wooden, Naval pivot carriage that was modified to center pintle, barbette.

100-pounder (6.4-inch) Parrott rifles in Battery Rosecrans, Morris Island, S.C. The gun on the left used an elevating screw, while that to its right employed a quoin. Bolts and shells lay about in the foreground; each came packed in its own individual shipping crate.

COLUMBIADS

The Columbiad was introduced to the United States service in 1811. Originally chambered, it combined features of the gun, howitzer, and mortar, and was our primary seacoast defense for many years. These smoothbores used during the Civil War were principally of the following types:

1. Model of 1844 — 8-inch and 10-inch. (Some of these were rifled and banded for added strength by the Confederates.)
2. Model of 1858 — 8-inch and 10-inch.
3. Model of 1861, "Rodman" Columbiad — 8-inch, 10-inch, and 15-inch. (One 20-inch was cast in 1864.)
4. Confederate copies of the "Rodman" — 8-inch and 10-inch.

The "Rodman" Columbiad was developed before the war by U. S. Ordnance Lieutenant (later Major) Thomas J. Rodman. The cast iron was poured into the mould around a water-cooled core, and simply this was the reason for their great strength. The "Rodman" is distinguished by its clean lines and notched, flat breech. Most U. S. Rodmans were mounted on iron carriages, while C. S. Rodmans are seen in contemporary photographs on wooden carriages. In defense of Northern cities and ports, it is probable that no 15-inch Rodmans ever fired a shot in anger.

	8-inch	10-inch	15-inch
Bore Diameter	8.0"	10.0"	15.0"
Tube Material	Iron	IronI	ron
Length of Tube	124"	126"	190"
Weight of Tube	9,210 lbs.	15,400 lbs.	50,000 lbs.
Weight of Shot	65 lbs.	128 lbs.	428 lbs.
Powder Charge	10 lbs.	18 lbs.	40 lbs.
Range at 5° Elevation	1,800 yds.	1,800 yds.	*

* At 25° Elevation with 300-pound shell and 50 pounds powder — 4,680 yards.

A battery of 10-inch "Rodman" Columbiads at Fortress Monroe, Va., 1863, mounted on wrought iron, center pintle, barbette carriages. The large cylinder attached to the rear of the first carriage may be an experimental apparatus to measure or lessen recoil.

The barbette tier of Fort Sumter mounted only 27 guns on April 12, 1861, of which eleven were 8- and 10-inch Columbiads. To protect his men, Major Anderson ordered that the exposed weapons on this level not be used during the bombardment. The cannon with its carriage's rear wheel appearing to touch the one gentleman's head is an 8-inch seacoast Columbiad on a wooden, center pintle, barbette carriage.

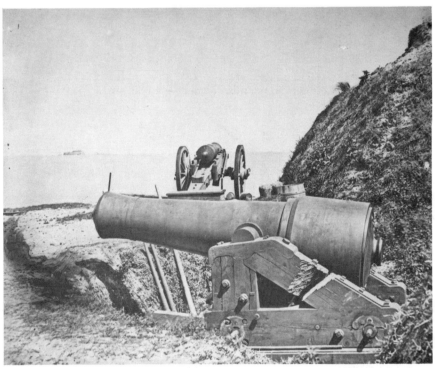

A photograph taken in 1865 after the Federal re-occupation of Charleston, S.C., shows two guns in Fort Johnson with Fort Sumter in the distance. The weapon in the background is an 8-inch siege & garrison howitzer, Model 1841, while that in the foreground is a 10-inch seacoast Columbiad, Model 1844, rifled and banded by the Confederates. Note that the Columbiad has been purposely dismantled by removing the truck wheels and cutting the brace with an axe.

A 15-inch "Rodman" Columbiad in Battery Rodgers, Alexandria, Va., mounted on a wrought iron, center pintle, barbette carriage.

Hauling a "Rodman" Columbiad through the streets of Washington, D.C., 1864.

MISCELLANEOUS

Norman Wiard, a U.S. Ordnance Department employee, invented several cannons that saw limited service during the Civil War. The tubes were cast "semi-steel" and, mounted on their specially designed carriages, were rather modern looking. Here, a section of Lt. Birchmeyer's Battery prepares to fire their 12-pounder Wiard smoothbores. Wiard rifles had a similar appearance and used Hotchkiss patent shot, shell and case.

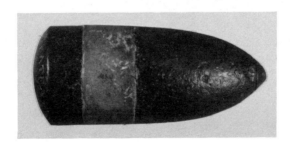

2.6-inch Hotchkiss shell for Wiard 6-pounder rifle
        Weight — 5 lbs.
        Diameter — 2.56"
        Length — 6.6"

Large caliber Parrott rifle mounted on a specially designed and built railway platform, photographed near Petersburg, Va.

During their occupation of Centreville, Va., in the winter of 1861-62, the Confederates shaped trees to generally resemble cannon barrels. These "Quaker" guns made the positions appear much stronger from a distance. The two views were taken in March 1862, after the Confederates had abandoned the works.

Three unidentified Union artillerymen — note the artillery sabres and accoutrements.

61

Northern manufactured artillery short sword with scabbard.

Two Confederate-made artillery short swords.

Federal sword belt plate (buckle) and belt with frog for the artillery short sword.

Sword belt plate and belt with hangers for the artillery sabre.

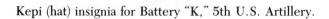

Kepi (hat) insignia for Battery "K," 5th U.S. Artillery.

Confederate artillery block "A" button (left), and Union eagle "A" artillery button (right).

ARTILLERY IMPLEMENTS

The artilleryman was issued a large number of implements with which to perform his tasks. These instruments were divided into classes depending on their specific use: pointing implements, loading implements, priming and firing implements, and general management implements.

Pointing Implements

QUADRANT — by the time of the Civil War it was used mostly with mortars or long, large-caliber guns. It measured the degree of elevation of the tube.

BREECH-SIGHT — the rear sight for aiming.

TANGENT SCALE — an early form of rear sight that measured elevation.

PENDULUM-HAUSSE — a free-swinging rear sight supported by a SEAT at the breech of the barrel. This was one of the better means for aiming.

MUZZLE-SIGHT — the front sight for aiming.

GUNNER'S LEVEL — used to determine the proper location for the breech-sight.

HANDSPIKE — a short wooden pole for moving the trail of the carriage either left or right. When not in use it was suspended on the cheek of the carriage.

QUOIN — a large wedge used in place of an elevating screw under the breech of mortars and some howitzers.

Breech sight for 20-pounder Parrott rifle

C.S. muzzle sight, top and side views

Gunner's level

Two muzzle sights

Pendulum-hausse

Seat for pendulum-hausse

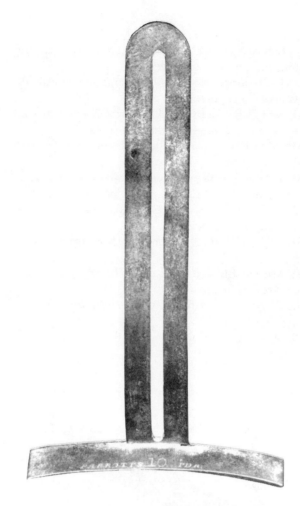

Breech sight for 10-pounder Parrott rifle

Loading Implements

RAMMER — a wooden staff with a head to force the powder charge and projectile into the barrel. When not in use it was suspended under the field carriage.

SPONGE — a woolen bag covering a wooden cylinder — for field pieces the sponge was attached to the opposite end of the same staff as the rammer. The sponge soaked in water extinguished sparks left after discharge and also helped remove black powder residue.

SPONGE-COVER — protected the sponge when not in use. It was usually made of canvas.

SHELL HOOKS — for loading shells not easily handled. The arms entered the "ears" to opposite sides of the fuse opening.

HAVERSACK — a leather bag used to transport the powder cartridge from the limber to the field cannon.

PASS-BOX — a wooden box used to transport the cartridge to siege and garrison pieces.

LADLE — used to remove unfired projectiles from the bore.

WORM — used to remove cartridge bags and rags from the bore.

SCRAPER — used to remove residue from the bore of mortars and howitzers.

Gunner's haversack

For Loading Shells

POWDER MEASURE — a copper utensil to measure bursting and propelling charges.

FUNNEL — for pouring bursting charges into the shell. It was made of copper.

FUSE SETTER — a brass cylinder which when struck, drove the wooden fuse plug into the shell.

FUSE MALLET — a wooden hammer for driving wooden fuse plugs.

FUSE SAW — a small saw for cutting wooden fuse plugs.

GUNNER'S CALLIPERS — used for measuring the length of time fuses, fuse plugs, the diameter of projectiles, and caliber of guns.

FUSE EXTRACTOR — for removing fuses from projectiles.

FUSE MEASURE — a board or block with graduations to measure fuse lengths.

FUSE PUNCH — for breaking into the Bormann time fuse powder train.

FUSE WRENCH — for setting metallic fuse plugs into projectiles.

Fuse measure

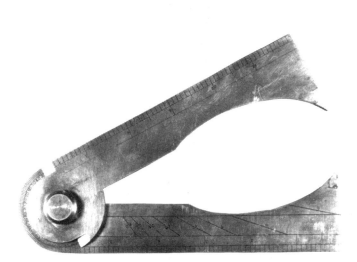

Gunner's callipers

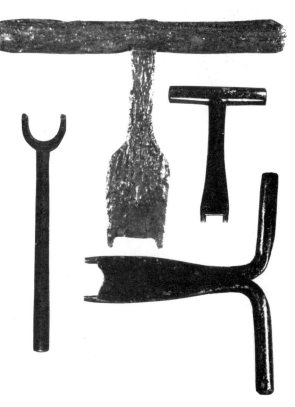

Four various fuse wrenches

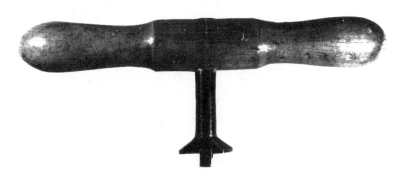

Fuse wrench for Bormann time fuse

Fuse punch for Bormann time fuse

Priming and Firing Implements

PRIMING WIRE — for piercing the cartridge bag prior to inserting the friction primer in the vent.

GIMLET —.for removing plugs or broken friction primers from the vent.

VENT-PUNCH — if the vent obstruction could not be removed with the gimlet, the vent punch was used to drive it into the bore.

GUNNER'S PINCERS — a combination pliers and nail puller for assorted uses.

LANYARD — a wooden handle to which was attached a twelve-foot cord, and a hook. The hook was inserted into the wire eye of the friction primer.

TUBE-POUCH — a leather pouch for carrying the lanyard, thumbstall, priming wire, gimlet, and friction primers. The tube pouch was worn on a leather belt around the waste.

THUMBSTALL — a buckskin cover for the thumb to protect it from heat while stopping the vent during loading. The string was tied securely around the wrist.

Thumbstall   Pincers

Priming wire   Lanyard

Gimlet   Vent punch

Confederate tube pouch made by J. Darrow, Augusta, Ga.

Federal tube pouch

General Management Implements

PROLONGE — a 26 foot 7 inch general purpose hemp rope carried on two hooks on the carriage trail when not in use.

VENT COVER — a leather strap to protect the vent when not in service. A brass or copper pin fastened to it with rivets entered the vent and prevented it from slipping.

TOW-HOOK — an iron hammer and hook for unpacking ammunition boxes and repairing sabot straps and fixed ammunition.

SPONGE BUCKET — an iron bucket for holding water into which the sponge was dipped.

TAR BUCKET — for transporting tar to be used as a lubricant for axles. It is more commonly known as a grease bucket.

WATER BUCKET — an oak bucket with iron hoops for carrying water in camp.

Tompion — for stopping the muzzle of a 12-pounder smoothbore when not in service.

Sponge bucket

Grease bucket

Water bucket

Library of Congress

Officers of Battery "A," 2nd U.S. Artillery photographed in the vicinity of Fair Oaks, Va., in June 1862: (left to right) Lt. Robert Clarke, Capt. John C. Tidball (commander), Lt. William H. Dennison, and Capt. Alex. C.M. Pennington. Note the arrangement of the implements on their 3-inch Ordnance rifle.

Assorted sponges for different caliber weapons

Tube pouch with priming wire on artilleryman's belt

SUMMARY OF FEDERAL PURCHASES AND FABRICATIONS

Summary statement of purchases and fabrications of artillery materiel by the Federal Ordnance Department from January 1, 1861, to June 30, 1866:

	Purchases	Fabrications	Total
Field guns	4,048	—	4,048
Siege guns	677	—	677
Seacoast guns	2,350	—	2,350
Mortars	817	—	817
Field carriages and limbers	2,416	1,360	3,776
Siege carriages and limbers	139	651	790
Seacoast carriages	391	1,863	2,254
Battery wagons, caissons and forges	3,326	931	4,257
Mortar beds	99	611	710
Projectiles for smoothbore guns	2,764,852	—	2,764,852
Projectiles for rifled guns	3,043,610	—	3,043,610
Pounds of grape and canister shot	6,539,999	—	6,539,999
Rounds of ammunition for smoothbore guns	146,514	1,527,649	1,674,163
Rounds of ammunition for rifled guns	8,543	1,179,471	1,188,014
Artillery harness, sets for two horses	18,858	9,306	28,164
Cartridge bags, filled	—	2,205,811	2,205,811
Friction primers	—	10,281,305	10,281,305
Fuses	—	4,226,377	4,226,377
Cannon powder, pounds	9,540,603	—	9,540,603
Mortar powder, pounds	7,428,142	—	7,428,142
Cartridge bags, unfilled	—	4,976,279	4,976,279
Cartridge bag stuff, yards	1,045,618	—	1,045,618

BIBLIOGRAPHY and SUGGESTED READING

Bartleson, John D. Jr., *Civil War Explosive Ordnance*. Washington, 1972.

Busey, John W. and Martin, David G., *Regimental Strengths at Gettysburg*. Baltimore, 1982.

Coggins, Jack, *Arms and Equipment of the Civil War*. New York, 1962.

Dickey, Thomas S. and George, Peter C., *Field Artillery Projectiles of the American Civil War*. Atlanta, 1980.

_____ , *The Field Manual for the Use of Officers on Ordnance Duty*. Richmond, 1862.

Frassanito, William A., *Grant and Lee, The Virginia Campaigns, 1864-1865*. New York, 1983.

Gibbon, John, *The Artillerist's Manual*. New York, 1860.

Hazlett, James C., Olmstead, Edwin, and Parks, M. Hume, *Field Artillery Weapons of the Civil War*. Newark, Del., 1983.

Kerksis, Sydney C. and Dickey, Thomas S., *Field Artillery Projectiles of the Civil War 1861-1865*. Atlanta, 1968.

Kerksis, Sydney C. and Dickey, Thomas S., *Heavy Artillery Projectiles of the Civil War 1861-1865*. Atlanta, 1972.

Lord, Francis A., *Civil War Collector's Encyclopedia*. Harrisburg, Pa., 1963.

Manucey, Albert, *Artillery Through the Ages*. Washington, 1949.

McKee, W. Reid and Mason, M. E. Jr., *Civil War Projectiles II*. 1975.

Miller, Francis T. (ed.), *The Photographic History of the Civil War*. New York, 1911.

Mordecai, Alfred, *Artillery for the United States Land Service*. Washington, 1849.

_____ , *The Ordnance Manual for the Use of the Officers of the United States Army*. Philadelphia, 1862.

Peterson, Harold L., *Round Shot and Rammers*. New York.

Ripley, Warren, *Artillery and Ammunition of the Civil War*. New York, 1970.

Vandiver, Frank E., *Ploughshares into Swords*. Austin, Tex. 1952.